KT-176-495

WHAT PEOPLE SAY
ABOUT STORYMAZE

'The whole story is really stupid and really funny!
I recommend everyone who needs a good laugh
to read this! It's totally crazy!'
Stephanie, *Lollipops Magazine*

'A dizzying confection of in-your-face narration,
knowing wit, cartoon strip and the glamorous world of
surfing... it's wild and it's wacky and it's great fun.'
Shelflife – Reading for Young People in Scotland

'Full of action, adventure, romance and
heaps of jokes – visual and verbal.'
Viewpoint

Other books in the **STORYMAZE** series

1. THE ULTIMATE WAVE
2. THE EYE OF ULAM
4. THE GOLDEN UDDER

STORYMAZE

3

THE WOODEN COW

written and illustrated by

TERRY DENTON

ALLEN&UNWIN

FOR MARY AND TIM

First published in 2002

Copyright © Terry Denton, 2002

All rights reserved. No part of this book may be reproduced or transmitted in any form or by any means, electronic or mechanical, including photocopying, recording or by any information storage and retrieval system, without prior permission in writing from the publisher. The Australian Copyright Act 1968 (the Act) allows a maximum of one chapter or ten per cent of this book, whichever is the greater, to be photocopied by any educational institution for its educational purposes provided that the educational institution (or body that administers it) has given a remuneration notice to Copyright Agency Limited (CAL) under the Act.

Allen & Unwin
83 Alexander St
Crows Nest NSW 2065
Australia
Phone: (61 2) 8425 0100
Fax: (61 2) 9906 2218
Email: info@allenandunwin.com
Web: www.allenandunwin.com
Visit Terry's website at: www.terrydenton.com

National Library of Australia
Cataloguing-in-Publication entry:

Denton, Terry, 1950– .
The wooden cow.

For children.
ISBN 1 86508 783 1.

I. Title. II. Title: Storymaze: the wooden cow.
(Series: Denton, Terry, 1950– Storymaze; 3).

A823.3

Cover and text design by Terry Denton and Sandra Nobes
Set in Helvetica by Sandra Nobes
Printed in Australia by McPherson's Printing Group, Maryborough, Victoria

10 9 8 7 6 5 4 3

1

WELL!!!

It is about time you opened this book.

I have been trapped in here for months.

Day after day, I hear you walk past the bookshelves with not even a thought for me. Meanwhile I lead a miserable life in the dark world of this unopened book, waiting, just waiting, for that glorious moment, the sudden jerk, the creaking of the pages, the blast of fresh air, the glare of light.

Some of my Narrator friends will never know that joy, locked forever in books nobody ever reads. I should be grateful to you, I suppose, for taking the time to open this book. But now I feel you are growing impatient to hear the story.

So let's get on with it!

*   *   *

'Claudia! Mikey! It's time to go,' calls Nico.

This is his big day. Nico has been in training for nine long, hard months for the 27th Annual World Surf Championships. This year he is sure he can win. He is sure he can win every year.

This year in particular he believes is his year. **The Year of Nico**.

Don't you just love optimists?

The comp is being held in Friesia, which is a surfers' paradise on the other side of the universe. Getting there would be a problem for you or for me, seeing as it's a couple of million light-years away. But Nico has a very nifty little device called M.I.T.

M.I.T. is a small, genetically engineered creature from the planet Duryllium. His name means Mental Image Transfer. And he is able to transfer you across the universe through space and time. Neat trick, eh?

To use M.I.T. is simple . . . and difficult.

You just take hold of him, form an image of your destination and . . . PLIK! . . . you disappear. A few moments later you reappear at your destination. Hopefully.

To master the mental image bit takes a lot of practice. But that's not the difficult part. Catching M.I.T. in a good mood . . . that's the tricky bit.

Nico, Claudia and Mikey collect all their surfing gear and hurry down to the beach. They take hold of M.I.T. and concentrate...

'To Friesia.'

PLIK!

2

'Where are you?' says Claudia, looking around. She can see M.I.T. but there's no sign of Nico and Mikey.

'We're here,' says Mikey. 'Where are *you*?'

Nico and Mikey are standing together, next to a high stone wall. They can't see Claudia or M.I.T. anywhere. But I know where they are. You see, I am the Narrator and I know everything.

They are in Friesia, which is where they wanted to be. Unfortunately M.I.T. has brought them there 4000 years too early. That's only a tiny error when you consider all the millions and millions of years that have been and ever will be.

But that's not their only problem. M.I.T. has brought them down near the wall of a city. Mikey and Nico are on one side of the wall and Claudia and M.I.T. are on the other. And it's a very tall wall.

9

10

3

Friesia is a small planet in the Bovine Galaxy. The Friesians are a peace-loving people who have lived for thousands of years in the one city on the planet, Friesia City.

They look a lot like the Friesian cows you may be used to seeing on Planet Earth. But they are different. For starters, they have humanoid bodies. You have to imagine that the universe is so vast that there is an infinite variety of everything, including Friesian cows.

While Friesian cows on Planet Earth stand around in fields all day eating grass, farting, burping and making milk, there are other very different types of Friesians elsewhere in the universe.

Once I visited a planet where there were no birds. Unfortunately there were thousands of full-sized Friesian cows flying around in the sky instead. It was a very messy and dangerous planet.

A Narrator friend told me about a planet somewhere in the Milky Way that has a very unusual form of Friesian cow. These cows have a body shaped like a fridge. In fact, these Friesians *are* part-fridge and part-cow. The good thing about that is that they fill themselves up with cartons of cold milk every day. So you never have to go out and buy more milk. Very handy.

*   *   *

But back to the story.

Claudia and M.I.T. are led away by the Friesian guards and taken to the Royal Palace. They are met by Amnesia, the Queen's secretary, who escorts them to the Royal Court.

'Your Royal Majesty, Queen Chateaubriand, Ruler of Greater Friesia,' announces Amnesia, 'I bring before you two creatures found loitering by the west wall.'

For those of you who don't speak Friesian, the Queen's name is pronounced *Shat-oh-bree-ond*. It means '*to be cooked in a vinegar and white wine sauce*'. Stupid name really. But I'm not going to be the one to tell the Queen that.

THE QUEEN OF FRIESIA.

14

The Queen turns to Claudia.

'**Who are you?**' she asks. '**And what are you doing in my city?**'

'My name is Claudia. I am a citizen of Ithaca. I landed here by mistake. But I have done nothing wrong. You have no reason to hold me. I insist you let me go.'

'**NO REASON TO HOLD YOU!**' says the Queen. '**You are a spy. That's reason enough.**'

'I am NOT a SPY!'

'**And that hideous creature that bit me? I'll have him barbecued on a skewer.**'

'You just scared him. He's hiding. I'll find him and then we'll go.'

'**You will stay here,**' shouts the Queen. '**You are my prisoner. In fact, we are all prisoners. We have an enemy at the gates. My city is under siege and has been for nine long months. No one can come in and no one can go out.**'

4

Back outside, Nico and Mikey bang on the huge wooden gates. Two guards look down from the parapet above.

'Go away!' they say.

'Let us in. We need to find our friends,' says Mikey.

'You can't come in.'

'But – '

'No buts. Town's closed to outsiders.'

Nico and Mikey argue with the guards for a while. But they get nowhere. Eventually they give up and wander off towards the beach. Dejected, they sit on the sand. There is no sign here of Nico's 27th Annual World Surf Championships. No crowds, no bunting, no surfers.

'I came here to win a tournament,' says Nico, 'and we can't even find it.'

'Yeah, that's a bit confusing,' says Mikey.

'Confusing? It's tragic!'

'We need to get hold of M.I.T.'

'But how?' asks Nico.

'Dunno,' says Mikey. 'We could wait for nightfall and climb over the walls?'

'I've already tried that,' says a voice. 'Too high, too slippery and too many guards.'

Nico and Mikey are startled.

A man walks out of the bushes. His name is Ulysses.

5

Ulysses tells Nico and Mikey his story. It seems that once upon a time he was lost and wandering in the mazes of the Underworld. He met this strange person. She called herself the Madame of the Maze.

She told Ulysses that some day he would undertake a journey to Friesia. There he would meet Queen Chateaubriand. They would fall in love at first sight. They would marry. And together they would rule Friesia for a hundred years.

So Ulysses gathered a band of men and sailed across the sky to Friesia. Unfortunately the Queen refused even to meet him.

'I will never allow a non-Friesian into my city,' she said.

But Ulysses refused to go home defeated. He and his men have been camping outside the city ever since. For nine long months he has refused to let any Friesians leave and *they* won't let *him* in. It is a stalemate.

'Why don't you just give up?' asks Nico.

'Because the Madame of the Maze told me that one day two strangers would magically appear. They would help me get into the city. They would bring me and my true love together.'

'You want to get closer to your true love, eh?' says Nico. 'I know how that feels.'

'You are those strangers,' says Ulysses, looking at Nico and Mikey. 'So what is your plan?'

'Plan?' says Mikey. 'We don't really have one.'

Ulysses looks disappointed.

'But we're working on it,' says Nico. 'True love must triumph.'

6

It is the morning after the day before. A stingy ray of sunlight struggles feebly down between the towers tall. Nico and Mikey are spying around the city walls, looking for a way in.

They have found a spot close to the cliff where the walls are much lower.

27

7

The Queen has given Claudia a room just near the Royal Bedroom, to keep a close eye on her. The Queen has decided she likes Claudia. Today she has invited her to play croquet at ten, have lunch at noon, do a spot of nightingale hunting at two and have dinner at 7 p.m. sharp.

Claudia wakes early. She dresses and sneaks out of her room. She tiptoes along the corridor.

'M.I.T.,' she hisses. She must find M.I.T. so that she can leave the city, find Nico and Mikey and get out of this parallel universe.

34

8

Back in Ulysses' camp, Mikey is helping Nico dry off after his unexpected swim.

'A Wooden Horse,' says Mikey, excitedly.

Ulysses and Nico look on, mystified.

'The dark shape I saw in the sea. That's what it was, a Wooden Horse.'

'So?' says Nico.

'What are we meant to do with a seahorse made of wood?' asks Ulysses.

But Mikey is not listening. There is an image forming in his head. The dark shape in the water has reminded him of something from his childhood.

He is sitting on the knee of his old white-haired mother, talking to her. But this is rather odd because Mikey's mother didn't have white hair. Maybe it's someone else's mother?

Now the image is clearer. The old white-haired mother has a beard. A white beard. She is asking Mikey whether he has been a good boy all year and does he deserve a present? Mikey suddenly realises he has the wrong image in his head.

(That is my fault, really. I lost my place in the story. In fact, I was reading the wrong story.)

Another image forms in Mikey's head. This time he is at school and his teacher is blathering on about myths and legends. She is telling the class the Ancient Greek story of the Wooden Horse of Troy.

I have prepared this stick-figure version for you.

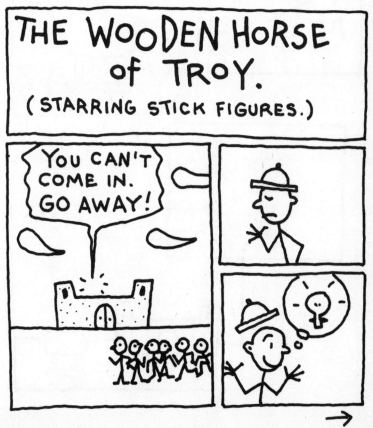

THE NEXT DAY.

THAT NIGHT.

38

9

'But, Ulysses, I'm surprised you haven't heard of the Wooden Horse of Troy?' says Mikey.

'Well, like everyone, I have read the famous stick-figure version of that story,' says the Big U. 'But I still don't get it.'

'In that stick-figure version,' says Mikey, 'the invaders got inside the Trojan city, hidden in the belly of a huge Wooden Horse.'

'But why was the Trojan city hidden in the belly of a horse?' asks Ulysses. 'That must have been some horse.'

'No, no,' says Mikey. 'You're not quite getting it yet, Ulysses. The Trojan city wasn't hidden in the belly of the horse, the soldiers were.'

'Oh, OK,' says Ulysses. 'That makes a lot more sense.'

It takes some time, but eventually Mikey manages to convince Ulysses that the Wooden Horse can get him into Friesia City.

'So,' says Mikey. 'All we need to do now is haul the horse out of the water.'

10

Well, I'll just flick ahead a few pages, as I know you're very busy.

Ulysses' men toil all day, hauling the Wooden Horse out of the sea. They dry it out and that night they set it up at the gates of Friesia City.

Then Ulysses' men dismantle their camp and hide in the bushes so the Friesians will think they have gone home.

11

'**Have some clover burgers,**' shouts the Queen to Claudia.

'Mmm, sounds appetising,' says Claudia, 'but I think I'll pass.'

The Queen is dining with Claudia.

'**Do you know of this man called Ulysses?**'

'Not really, Your Majesty, only what I have read at school. Have *you* ever met him?'

'**No, I've never met him. But I have heard many stories about him. He is said to be brave, and strong, and funny. Although some say he's not too bright.**'

'Sounds like most Ithacan men. Would you like to meet him, Your Majesty?'

'**Yes, I guess I would. It's lonely being Queen, you know, Claudia. I'd like a boyfriend, but I just know he would barge in and take over the place. And I don't want to give up my throne. I love being Queen. But I don't want to spend the rest of my life alone, either. What's a Queen to do?**'

'You could pass the yoghurt, Your Majesty.'

12

Two guards are on duty on the walls of Friesia City. They are standing on a dingy little platform where a stingy ray of sunlight struggles feebly down between the towers tall.

'Cold morning, Gordon.'

'Derek, I already know it is a cold morning. My hands are numb, my nose is like concrete, I can't feel my toes and when my breath leaves my mouth it turns into iceblocks.'

'It's never as cold on Duryllium, Gordon.'

You may remember these two guards. They are Derek and Gordon of Duryllium and we met them in *The Ultimate Wave*. Since then, they have been banished from their home planet by Prince Icon and are destined to spend the rest of their lives in exile.

'Derek, did I not tell you not to talk about Duryllium?'

'Excuse me, Gordon. I did not quite under-stand what you said just then,' says Derek. 'Did you say: *Did I not tell you not to talk about*

Duryllium? Or *Did I not tell you not to not talk about Duryllium?'*

'SHUT UP, DEREK!!! The Friesians might overhear us. Just don't mention our beloved homeland, OK?

'Just trying to make conversation, Gordon.'

'Well, don't.'

While Gordon snivels beside him, Derek looks down. He can make out a dark shape in the misty light.

'Gordon, what's that?'

'What's what, Derek?'

'What's that, down there?' says Derek.

They both shuffle to the edge of the parapet and look down.

'Great Captain Crundor!' they chorus.

Before them stands a huge horse.

'It's ... It's ... '

'It's a huge horse, Derek,' says Gordon. 'Don't look at it. It might go away.'

'But it's a huge horse, Gordon,' says Derek.

'We're off duty in another hour, Derek. Don't say anything and we'll leave it to the next watch to sort out.'

'But it's a HUGE HORSE, Gordon. We have to tell someone.'

'Derek, keep your voice down. If we don't see it, then it doesn't exist,' says Gordon.

'But it's a HUGE HORSE, Gordon.'

'What is all the commotion about?' says Amnesia, the Queen's secretary, marching onto the parapet. 'What's this about a horse?'

'A really HUGE horse!' says Derek.

'Quiet, Derek,' Gordon hisses.

But it is too late. In a very short time, the city gates swing open and a whole bunch of officials and guards and Friesian citizens are wandering about looking at the really huge horse. They are feeling its legs and running their hands over its flanks and there is a lot of discussion about what a really huge horse is doing at the gates of their city. And whether they should bring it inside. And whether it should run in the Friesian Cup on the first Tuesday in November.

13

I don't know how you feel about the number 13.
But I am deeply suspicious of it. My cat was run
over on the 13th day of the 13th month, just
after she had had 13 kittens.

I was so sad. I couldn't bear to part with her
fluffy little babies, so I kept them all. They grew
into cats, all of them female. Eventually all 13
cats became pregnant.

Each cat had 13 female kittens. Now I had
182 cats. It wasn't easy feeding 182 cats, I can
tell you.

I didn't want any more kittens so I spent
a lot of time eliminating all the tomcats in my
neighbourhood. But somehow, next spring, all
182 cats became pregnant.

They had 13 female kittens each. Meaning
I had 2548 cats and I had to clean up after
2548 cats. Each day a truck dumped 10 cubic
metres of cat gravel at my place. That's 70
cubic metres a week.

Mrs Narrator tried spreading the used cat
gravel on her roses. But you need a lot of

roses for 70 cubic metres of poo-filled cat gravel.

Then all the cats got pregnant again. They had 13 female kittens each.

Now I was up to my armpits in 35,672 cats! They were eating me out of house and home. There was a mountain of cat gravel in the backyard. And next spring they all got pregnant again!

So don't talk to me about 13.

I hate 13.

That's why there is no Chapter 13 in this book.

(By the way, I have a nice recipe for cat risotto if anyone is interested.)

14

A dark figure suddenly appears in the gateway.

The citizens of Friesia turn and gasp.

Yes, they all gasp in shock and horror at exactly the same time.

Now I know that sounds unlikely, but I'm the Narrator and I tell you that's exactly what happened.

'What's all the commotion about?' shouts a deep and regal voice. It is voice of the Queen of Friesia, which comes out of the mouth of the Queen of Friesia, which is a huge opening on the head of the Queen of Friesia. She is not happy about being woken at dawn. She is tired. She was up late last night plucking nightingales in her garden.

'This horse has magically appeared, Your Majesty,' says Amnesia. 'And Ulysses' camp is empty.'

Claudia looks closely at the horse. She runs her hands over its flanks. Did you know that Claudia and Mikey went to the same school? They were in the same grade. Claudia remembers the Wooden Horse story too.

She decides this is a Mikey-inspired trick to get inside the city to rescue her. She figures Nico and Mikey are inside this horse. Claudia wants to tap a message on the horse's flanks, but she doesn't want to make the Queen suspicious.

'This could be an offering to the gods,' she says. 'It could mean Ulysses has given up and gone home, and left you a parting gift.'

'Is that what you think?' shouts the Queen, watching Claudia very closely. She is still not sure if she can trust Claudia. She still has a faint suspicion she might be one of Ulysses' spies.

'It looks harmless,' says Claudia.

'Amnesia? What do you think?'

'I . . . I can't remember,' says Amnesia.

The Queen is deep in thought. Finally she shouts: **'I agree with Claudia. Haul the horse inside.'**

15

The Queen of Friesia stands on a ceremonial platform near a low part of the city wall. Before her is the huge Wooden Horse, which the citizens of Friesia are festooning with flowers.

Have you ever festooned anything? I have. Every Christmas, I festoon my house with festoons. And for Mrs Narrator's birthday lunch in June I do a bit of festooning too. She loves festooned balloons. In fact, she loves to get a balloon strewn with festoon at noon in June.

But that's another matter!

Back to the Queen.

'**I, the Queen of Friesia, welcome this beautiful and mysterious gift. This Wooden Horse is a celebration of my beauty and wisdom.**'

The people cheer and sing.

'**QUIET! I haven't finished! I declare this horse an offering to the gods.**'

The people start cheering and singing.

'**QUIET! I still haven't finished! We must**

welcome it and celebrate it in the time-honoured Friesian way.'

The Queen lights incense at the base of the huge Wooden Horse, which is a signal for children in black-and-white spotted costumes to start dancing around the horse, singing sacred songs.

MEANWHILE INSIDE THE WOODEN HORSE.

55

The Queen stands up to speak. The children stop their singing and dancing. The crowd falls silent.

'**Now let us return this offering to the gods.**'

The people cheer and move forward, pushing the Wooden Horse towards the back of the platform.

16

17

(I apologise for the previous chapter. It was on loan from another book and should have been returned some weeks ago. Read this chapter instead.)

18

I apologise for that Chapter 17 which you may have noticed appeared to be completely blank. In fact it wasn't. It's just that the words were printed in extremely small type so they were very, very hard to see. But, don't fret, you haven't missed anything much. Except that our heroes have decided that although the Wooden Horse didn't work, a Wooden Cow just might. It was Nico's brainwave.

*   *   *

So, the morning after the day before, Ulysses and his men haul the Wooden Horse out of the sea again and start to rework it as a cow. They paint it white all over, then add a few big black spots, different ears and a couple of horns.

'By Hades, that even looks like a cow,' says Ulysses. 'But there's something missing.'

'Yes, it needs a rudder, says Nico.

'I think you mean an udder,' says Ulysses. 'Cows need udders.'

'No, if the cow works as well as the horse did, and they throw it in the sea, we're going to need a rudder.'

'Holy gods of the Underworld,' says Ulysses, 'where are we going to find a large-scale false udder out in the wilderness on this godforsaken beach?'

Good question, that one. Where *do* you find an udder when you need one? It's easy if you're a cow. It'd just be there, underneath you. Wherever you went, it would follow.

But if you're not a cow, and most of us aren't, then it's a bit more difficult.

Ulysses looks up 'udder' on his laptop. There are a couple of million matches. Ulysses scrolls through the list: Udder Delight, Udder Nonsense, Udders on Toast, Death by Udder, Udder Cruelty, Udder Club (must be something you hit cows with), Udders with Rubbers, and so on and so forth. Then there is the site Ulysses has been looking for.

'YEESSS!' says Ulysses. 'Udders.r.us.com. We'll just order one, size 22 – an all-pink, rubber cow's udder – for instant delivery anywhere in the universe, $49.95 plus packaging and handling. Just punch in my credit card details. And Bob's your uncle.'

19

Later that afternoon, Ulysses and his men are adding the finishing touches to the cow, when they hear the jingling of bells. A few minutes later a cart and donkey appear, driven by a man dressed all in tartan. He jumps down from the cart.

'Ahoy, yon warriors,' he calls.
Ulysses strides over to the newcomer.
'Who in the Pantheon are you?'
'My name is Hamish McHaggis. And I believe you just ordered an udder. It just so happens that udders are my specialty.'

He walks around to the back of the cart and pulls out a huge rubber udder and hands it to Ulysses.

22

A stingy ray of sunlight struggles feebly down between the towers tall. Yet another dawn!

'Gordon, do you see what I see?'

'No, Derek, I don't. There is nothing there.'

'But, I can see a – '

'Just look the other way.'

Derek and Gordon turn and look in the other direction.

Nico sneaks a peek out of the cow's door.

'Those guards are ignoring us,' says Nico.

'Keep your voice down, we don't want them to hear us,' whispers Ulysses.

There is a bit of thinking time in the Wooden Cow. Then Mikey takes a deep breath and forms his hands into a sort of horn around his mouth.

'MMMMMOOOOOOOOOO!!!'

There is no response.

'MMMMMOOOOOOOOOO!!!' Still nothing.

'MMMMMOOOOOOOOOO!!!'

Slowly, the gates of the city swing open and out steps Amnesia.

'You guards up there! Did I just hear a giant cow?'

Derek and Gordon take no notice. They continue to look the other way.

In a short time, a huge throng gathers outside the city gates.

'Nice udder,' says the Queen, striding around the huge Wooden Cow. **'Is this another gift from Ulysses, Claudia?'**

'No!' says Claudia, who wants to avoid the Wooden Cow being thrown off the cliff again. 'No, this looks like something different.'

'No I'm sure it is a gift for the People of Friesia from that stupid Ulysses. We must festoon it and return it to the gods.'

'No,' says Claudia, 'why not keep it as a memorial to your great victory over Ulysses?'

But the Queen is convinced. She rises up before them and declares this day will henceforth be known as the Day of the Wooden Cow.

The Friesians cheer and drag the Wooden Cow to the ceremonial platform. They do some of their best festooning. And the children dance around the Wooden Cow singing songs that praise the glorious Day of the Wooden Cow. Others draw beautifully coloured Wooden Cow pictures and pin them on the side of the giant Wooden Cow.

I have prepared this stick-figure version of what happened next. It should save you a bit of time.

23

Ulysses and his men sit around the camp
drying out. Tears well up in Ulysses' eyes as
he struggles to talk to his men.

'Boys, I think this is the end. Time we all
went back home.'

'What about a Wooden Cattle Dog?' says
Nico.

'What?' says Mikey.

'We could haul the cow out of the sea and
give it a cattle dog makeover,' says Nico. 'Tell
me the Friesians could resist a giant Wooden
Cattle Dog.'

'No, boys, I'm done with giant wooden
things. I've had enough.'

'Ahoy, yon miserable warriors!' Hamish
McHaggis steps forward. 'Do I have a deal for
you!'

McHaggis announces that he can get
Ulysses into the city and help him win the
heart of the Queen of Friesia. But there will
be a price.

'There is an Udder room in the palace,' says McHaggis. 'And in that room there is a Golden Udder. I want you to steal the Golden Udder and bring it back to me.'

'Sure,' says Ulysses. 'You give me the Queen and I'll gladly give you the Udder.'

'But if you fail to give me the Golden Udder, I will put a curse on you. On your wedding day, the Queen will look into your eyes and see a fool. She will throw you out of Friesia. And then, Ulysses, you will be doomed to a life of misery and torment in the Underworld.'

'Hmmm,' says Ulysses, 'maybe I should . . . '

'But if you do deliver to me the Golden Udder, you will know only happiness and joy with the Queen of your heart.'

'Well, OK. That sounds really good.' So Ulysses seals the deal with Hamish McHaggis.

What McHaggis doesn't want Ulysses to know is that he desperately needs the Golden Udder, an ancient symbol of Might and Power. McHaggis is being punished for his many bad deeds. A servant of the gods of the Underworld, he is free to come and go, but he is always at their beck and call. He desperately wants to free himself of their power. The Golden Udder will do this for him. But he's not going to tell Ulysses that. Not that Ulysses could care.

He is obsessed only with winning the Queen's heart... at any price.

'So,' says Ulysses, 'what's your plan, McHaggis?'

'Give me two men and three days and I'll have you inside that Friesian city,' says McHaggis. 'Or is that three men and two days?'

'Oh, sure! We've been trying for nine long months to get in there. What makes you think you can do it in three days?'

'McHaggis's First Law,' he announces. 'If you want to capture their hearts, then first you must capture their stomachs. It never fails.'

24

Standing beside the Burger Machine, McHaggis opens a tiny door in the side.

'Just pop in here and join your friends, Mr Ulysses,' he says, 'and when you next emerge you will be inside the gates of the Friesian city.'

With that, Ulysses' men hurry away to hide in the bushes, and await their leader's call.

25

A stingy ray of sunlight struggles feebly down between the towers tall.

Outside the gates of Friesia stands a proud Hamish McHaggis. Next to him is his masterpiece, a giant Wooden Cow Mobile Burger Bar Vending Machine. Try and say that quickly ten times! Inside, Nico and Mikey have fired the burners and are cooking up some tasty treats. The superchargers on the exhaust fans push the smell of cooking deep inside the Friesian city.

'Gordon, do you smell that beautiful smell?' says Derek.

'Certainly not, Derek,' says Gordon.

'That irresistible sumptuous greasy meaty perfume ... '

A sumptuous greasy meaty perfume?

That can only mean one thing. Hamish McHaggis has convinced Ulysses to sign up to a deal setting up the first Haggis Burger Bar franchise on this planet.

Have you ever eaten a Haggis Burger? It is made from 100% genuine haggis. And haggis, for those of you who aren't deranged enough to have eaten any in the past, is a traditional Scottish dish made from the chopped up heart, lung and liver of a lamb blended with fat, porridge and a mixture of 178 different herbs and spices. Sound tasty?

Haggis is usually cooked and served in the stomach of a sheep. Yum! But this is where McHaggis was very clever. He realised people are not big on sheep-stomach eating. So he had this idea to bung his Haggis Burgers between two halves of a crispy hot buttered bun.

'As soon as those stubborn Friesians get one whiff of my Haggis Burgers, you'll be inside their city quicker than a six-legged greyhound. This I guarantee,' whispers McHaggis.

'**What the . . . ?**' shouts the Queen, streaming through the city gates. She stops before the large brightly coloured machine.

'Welcome, Your Majesty,' says McHaggis.

'**What is that delicious aroma?**' The Queen's nostrils are all a-quiver.

'That tantalising aroma, my fair Queen, wafts forth from a genuine Hamish McHaggis Haggis Burger, the latest taste sensation from the kitchens of the Underworld.'

McHaggis takes a shiny gold coin out of his pocket and slips it into the machine.

'Let yourself be the first of the Fair Friesian Folk to masticate on this tongue taster,' he says to the Queen.

The Wooden Cow Mobile Burger Bar lights up, plays a bit of a tune, clunks, hisses and eventually spits out a steaming Haggis Burger in a neat and colourful dolphin-skin box.

The Queen's cow-like nostrils are flaring so much you could drive a VW through them. A small VW, that is. Large gobs of saliva appear around her mouth, glistening in the soft morning sunlight. Her eyeballs enlarge. She leans towards McHaggis, grabs the burger and in an instant it is gone. Swallowed, that is.

'That was nice,' says the Queen. **'Very nice! Let me try another.'**

She downs another just as quickly. This time the paper napkin disappears with it. And a sauce sachet.

In a short time the Queen demolishes eleven Haggis Burgers. For some people that would be a fatal dose, but not for the Queen of Friesia.

'Something to wash it down with?' suggests Hamish McHaggis, handing the Queen a cold bottle of Gorgon Cola. She downs that just as quickly, spitting out the empty bottle.

'BBBAAARRRPPP!' She lets out such a

loud burp that it causes a few stones to fall from the city wall.

'I am allowed to do that,' she says, **'I'm Queen.'**

Gorgon Cola for those of you who have never drunk it, comes from the Gorbachev Peninsula. It is a fizzy, purply-green drink. Very tasty indeed. It is made from the fermented toenail extract of the gigantic Gorgons of Goree Island.

While that may not sound appealing, it is a surprisingly refreshing drink. Really, it is one of those things you just have to try. Like haggis. And sheep's stomach.

Anyway, moving right along.

The Queen gives her Royal Approval to the Mobile Burger Bar and orders that it be brought inside the city gates. McHaggis tries to follow, but Amnesia blocks his way.

'Sorry, pal, Friesians only,' she says, slamming the doors on him.

'But that's my cow ...' he screams, and many other things as well. But the Friesians won't let McHaggis in.

Meanwhile the Friesians are stuffing coins into the machine as fast as they can, and Haggis Burgers are flying out the other end just as quickly.

Inside the Burger Bar, Nico and Mikey are struggling to keep up with the demand. Ulysses, who has been resting up at the back end of the cow, puts on an apron and starts to help out. He quite enjoys it actually.

26

Late that night, Claudia lies in bed. She can't sleep. There is a faint knocking sound, like a deranged woodpecker, coming from outside. She has piled all her pillows over her head, but she can't block out the persistent knocking.

'**That's it!**' she says, storming out of her room, down the corridor and out into the courtyard.

The Wooden Cow Burger Bar Vending Machine stands there, silent in the moonlight. Well, almost silent. Claudia follows her ears, which is very hard to do. You ought to try it sometime.

The knocking is coming from inside the cow.

'You dingbats! You've locked yourselves inside, haven't you?'

'Mmmpphh. Ooomppphh.Mmmfffrrrppp,' comes a reply from inside the cow.

Claudia opens the door and Nico, Mikey and Ulysses tumble out.

'Um, er ... thanks,' says Ulysses.

'Don't mention it,' Claudia laughs, 'you idiots.'

'You blokes stay here,' says Ulysses. 'I'll open the gates and let McHaggis in.'

Ulysses moves across the courtyard like a shadow in the night. So does his shadow. He slips gracefully under a cart, and leaps over a small fence. Unfortunately he lands right in the goose pen.

HONK! HONK! **HONK! HONK!** HONK! **HONK! HONK!** HONK! HONK! HONK! **HONK!** HONK! **HONK!** HONK! HONK! **HONK!** HONK! HONK! HONK! HONK! HONK! HONK! **HONK!** HONK! **HONK!** HONK! HONK! **HONK!** HONK! HONK! **HONK!**

The geese wake up. And so does the entire planet.

27

'Quick, follow me,' says Claudia, leading the others back into the palace. 'We can hide in my room.'

They rush up a corridor and turn left. They can hear guards chasing behind them.

'Hurry!'

'Stop!' says Ulysses. 'I can hear guards in front of us too.'

They stop by a door.

'Quick, in here,' says Ulysses. They rush into the room and close the door. The guards meet in the corridor. They argue and shout and finally all run off again.

'Holy Occhilupo!' says Nico.

'Quiet, Nico, the guards will hear us.'

'But look . . .'

They all turn around.

It's the Queen. She is sitting on her mini-throne, holding a sword. She is not alone. The room is full of guards. Ulysses and the Ithacans are captured.

28

But now an amazing thing happens. When Ulysses is brought before the Queen, their eyes meet. And just like in the prophecy, they fall in love at first sight. The Queen drops her sword and rushes into Ulysses' arms. They kiss. Then they kiss again. And again. And again. They kiss for hours.

Everyone else has to stand around watching them kiss. All except Claudia, who happens to see M.I.T. hiding in the shadows on the other side of the room.

29

The Queen is delirious with love. She welcomes
Ulysses and his friends and grants them the
freedom of the palace. When eventually she is
called away to her duties, Ulysses rushes off to
find the Ithacans.

'We have to get the Udder,' he explains to
Claudia.

'Why?' asks Claudia.

'It's just the way it has to be. We made a
deal.'

'You made a deal,' says Claudia.

'McHaggis got us into the city,' says Mikey.
'We promised him the Golden Udder.'

'The Queen will be furious!'

'We must keep our word, Claudia.'

'OK, but I'm not happy about it.'

Ulysses leads them through the palace.
They stop outside a door. Ulysses smiles. He
checks to make sure no one is looking and
opens the door. He pushes them all inside and
gently closes the door behind him.

'What a beauty,' declares Ulysses.

He is looking at the Golden Udder, sitting

on a pedestal, shining out in all its golden udderiness.

'This will bring a smile to McHaggis's face,' says Ulysses.

'And get you off the hook,' says Claudia.

Ulysses reaches forward and takes the Golden Udder off the pedestal.

'Now you must do something for me,' says Ulysses to the Ithacans.

'We seem to be doing a lot for you,' says Claudia, 'you great beefcake.'

'But you must take this to McHaggis. He's waiting for it beyond the city gates.'

'Why must we?' says Claudia.

'Because I have something you want.' Ulysses pulls a towel out of his backpack.

'101100.' The towel is wriggling.

'M.I.T.,' calls Claudia, reaching out for him. But Ulysses pulls M.I.T. away.

'Not so fast. You can have him back, but I want your solemn promise that you will deliver the Golden Udder to McHaggis. Then he'll lift his curse off my back and the Queen will love me forever. You must do this for me.'

'I do,' says Nico. 'I mean, we will.' Ulysses hands the Udder to Nico.

Suddenly the door bursts open. Guards run

in and surround the Ithacans and Ulysses. The Queen follows.

'What's going on here?' she shouts.

Things happen very quickly at this point. So quickly even the type is too blurry to read. The Queen has caught the Ithacans red-handed stealing her sacred Golden Udder.

'This is the supreme symbol of my Might and Power. How could you . . .?'

Now Ulysses thinks very quickly, for once. He realises that his chance of love with the Queen is doomed if McHaggis doesn't get the Golden Udder. Ulysses thinks he just might be able to talk the Queen around. He throws M.I.T. to Claudia.

'Go,' he says.

Claudia realises she has only a few seconds to act. She grabs the hands of her friends and whispers:

'To the city gates.'

PLIK!

The Ithacans disappear.

30

PLIK!

M.I.T. takes them to the front gate. Only it's about 4000 years later.

There is no McHaggis waiting for them. He's long dead. So are the Queen and Ulysses. In fact, there are no city gates either. Nor is there a Friesian city any more, just a big pile of stones.

'M.I.T., what have you done?' yells Claudia, but she is too confused to be really angry with him.

'Now what do we do?' says Nico, still holding on to the Golden Udder.

'Can you get us back to that exact moment in time again, M.I.T.?' says Mikey.

'100011.'

I reckon that's a no.

'What's that noise?' asks Claudia.

There's some sort of commotion on the beach. They run over to investigate.

'Nico! It's the Surf Comp.'

'NNNOOOOO!!!' screams Nico. He is

pointing to the podium, where Hercules is standing proud and tall holding the winner's cup. Nico's archenemy has won the World Surf Championship.

This is too much for Nico.

He grabs the M.I.T. and his friends' hands and screams: 'To Ithaca.'

PLIK!

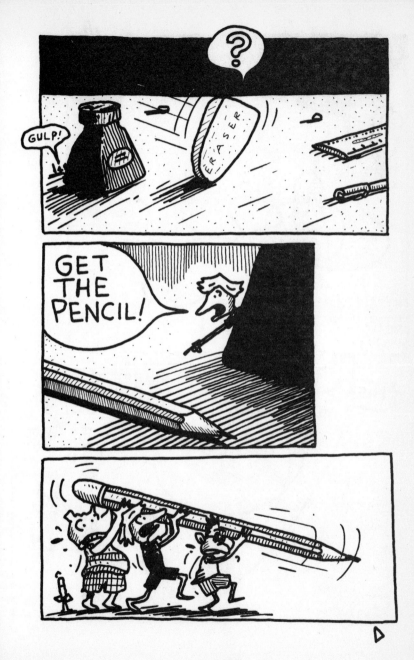

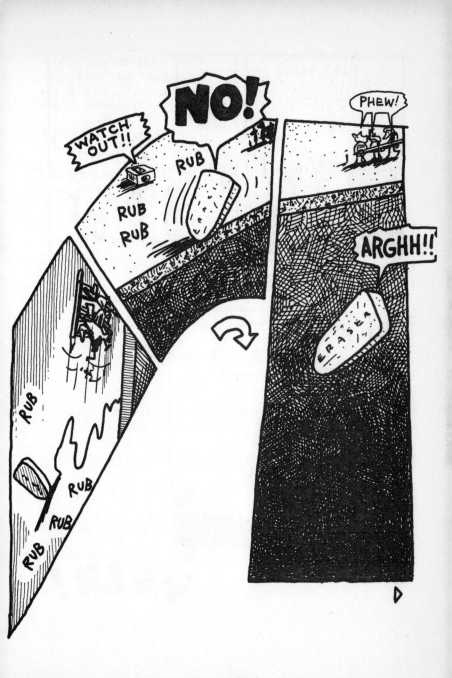

31

32

A stingy ray of sunlight struggles feebly down between the clouds so tall, lighting up a beach on Ithaca.

Nico, Claudia and Mikey are watching the sunset. Nico's friends are trying to console him.

'And what about that stupid Udder?' says Claudia. 'I told you to drop it, you blockhead.'

'And when have I ever listened to you?'

'What if they come looking for it? What about poor Ulysses and his Queen?'

'But that was thousands of years ago,' says Nico. 'They are all long gone. Who's going to want the Golden Udder now?'

Nico hands around a drink jug filled with ice and an unlimited supply of Gorgon Cola . . . unlimited because once you've had one sip of Gorgon Cola, you'll never want another. The drink jug looks remarkably like a Golden Udder.

'Claudia,' says Nico, 'without Mikey and me, you'd probably still be in Friesia right now, chasing M.I.T. around that palace and playing croquet with the Queen.'

'Grrrr!' says Claudia. 'Fat chance.'

'You must be so grateful to us, your saviours.'

'GGGRRR! In your dreams, Nico.'

'We're out of Gorgon Cola, Claudia. Show us your gratitude and fill this up,' says Nico, handing Claudia the Golden Udder.

'Are you sure it's empty, Nico?' says Claudia, standing up. 'Maybe you should have a close look.'

KLUNK!!

33

The Last Chapter

And that, dear reader, is the end of my tale. Which is why it's the last chapter.

So I suppose you will just close the book now and put it away on the shelves. And there I will remain until someone else decides to open it up again.

But don't you worry about me. You have your own life to lead. I don't want to hold you back. You must move on. There will be other books. Other bookshelves. Other great libraries to discover. It's an exciting world out there. Seize the day!

Go on. You know what you have to do.

Just close the book and walk away. Don't look back.

Do it, but be gentle.

Close the book, I'm ready.

Just close the –

A GUIDE TO M.I.T.'S* LANGUAGE

1	I hate surfing
0	There's lice in here!
00	I'm too young to die
01	You idiot!
10	I hate sand
11	Bummer
000	Oh,OH!
001	OH, NO!
010	Hello
011	Goodnight
100	Welcome back, goanna-head
101	Pooh!
110	Ouch!
111	ZZZZZ
0000	My yak has fleas
0001	HELP!
0010	Oh, joy
0011	Go away
0100	That's handy
0101	You double idiot
0110	Why me?
1000	Hee hee
1011	His feet stink
1100	What about my TV?
1111	I'm outta here
00000	My head hurts
00001	It's not my fault
00011	That would hurt
00100	This is nice!
00101	This is serious!
00110	The roof is leaking

00111	Hello, ugly!
01001	Hold my hand
01010	Can't make me
01100	Not telling
01110	Bye, bye
01111	GRRRR!
10001	Die, you fiend!
10010	Get this smelly lump off me
10101	Just following orders
10111	Panic stations!
11000	Hello, strange animal-headed people
11011	Smarter than you, lizard-brains
11111	HEE HEE HEE
100000	It's only a flesh wound
100011	I want my mummy
100101	Just following orders, fly-breath
100111	Quiet, you stupid animal-headed people
101001	Can't catch me!
101010	Put me down!
101100	Let me go!
110001	You smell, lizard-brains!
110010	Holy Occhilupo, you're ugly
110011	Get your bottom off my leg
110101	Holy Occhilupo!
110110	Gulp!
110111	The whole world's turned dark
111001	My feet are on fire
111010	I hate water
111011	@%&#$*!!
111100	NNNOOO!
111101	The kettle's boiling
1110111	Yes!

*M.I.T. (pronounced *em-eye-tee*) is short for Mental Image Transfer.

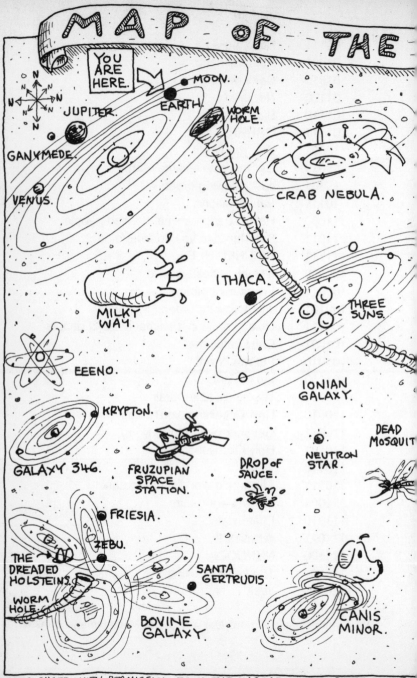

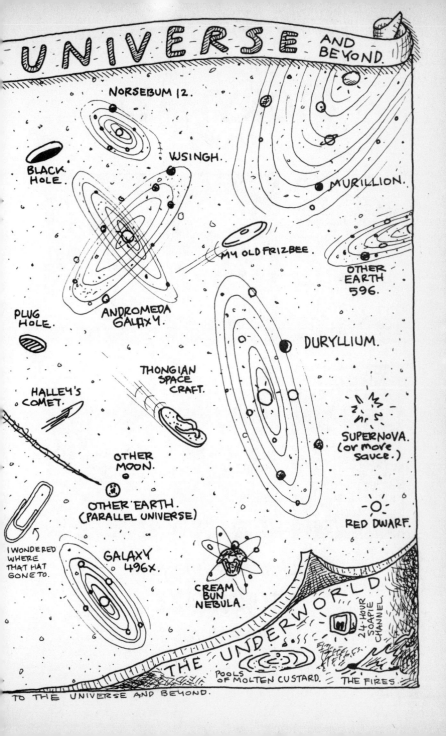

COLLECT THE
STORYMAZE
SERIES!

Look out for the next
STORYMAZE
adventure!